"It is not what we
have that will make
us a great nation;
it is the way in
which we use it."

To Bob and his boys, David, Peter, and Rory
—D.R.

I dedicate this book to the love, guidance, and memories
of my mother and father.
—C.F.P.

This book is set in Mrs. Eaves and Baskerville Semibold.

First Edition
10 9 8 7 6 5 4 3 2 1
F850-6835-5-13196
Printed in Singapore
Reinforced binding

ISBN 978-1-4231-2488-7
Library of Congress Cataloging-in-Publication Data is available.
Visit www.disneyhyperionbooks.com

# TO DARE MIGHTY THINGS

The Life of
**Theodore Roosevelt**

*by* **Doreen Rappaport**

*illustrated by* **C. F. Payne**

Disney • Hyperion Books
New York

"Teedie," as he was called,
coughed, sneezed, wheezed,
had raging fevers, and hardly ate.
His asthma was so bad he had to sleep
sitting up in bed or in a big chair.

Until he got glasses, he could only
see things very close up.
But that didn't stop him from
studying photographs for hours
of hippopotami with canoes on their backs
and zebras racing across the African plains.
He gobbled up books about
the soldiers at Valley Forge and
frontiersmen Davy Crockett and Daniel Boone.

"I felt a great admiration for men who were fearless.
I had a great desire to be like them."

Teedie stuffed hedgehogs into drawers.
Sometimes they escaped.
Guests were warned to check water pitchers
for snakes before pouring.

"He has to be watched all the time,"
his mother told his father.

He illustrated and wrote books about
ants, spiders, ladybugs, fireflies,
hawks, minnows, and crayfish.
His fingers were always stained with ink.
He collected animal and bird specimens
and created a museum in his room.
He smelled. The whole house smelled.

"All growing boys tend to be grubby; but the ornithological boy is the grubbiest of all."

His father told him,

# "You have the mind, but not the body.
# You must make your body."

Never one to not meet a challenge,
Teedie took hikes, pressed weights,
and swung up and down on bars.
His skinny chest and muscles grew.
But he was still sickly.

That didn't stop him from
climbing mountains and volcanoes,
hunting jackals on horseback, and
camping in subfreezing weather.
He noted every experience
in his diary.

He wanted to go to college but
worried that he didn't have the energy.
A tutor prepared him at home.
He crammed three years of study into two.

# "Is it not splendid! I passed, in all the eight subjects I tried."

He couldn't bring his museum to Harvard,
so he created a new one in his room there.
His giant tortoise escaped its pen and
terrified his landlady.

He studied long hours.
But he still found time to
box, wrestle, hunt, ice-skate,
teach Sunday school, and
dance away the nights at fancy balls.

Instead of resting in the summer,
he researched and wrote a book
about ninety-seven different birds.

# "Looking back over my eighteen years, I have never spent an unhappy day, unless by my own fault."

At twenty, he fell in love
with Alice Hathaway Lee,
who gave him the nickname Teddy.
But before marrying, he went West to hunt.
His doctor had told him not to go.
He had to live a quiet life or he would die soon.

## "If I've got to live that sort of life, I don't care how short it is."

He went away for three weeks.

## "By Godfrey, this is fun!"

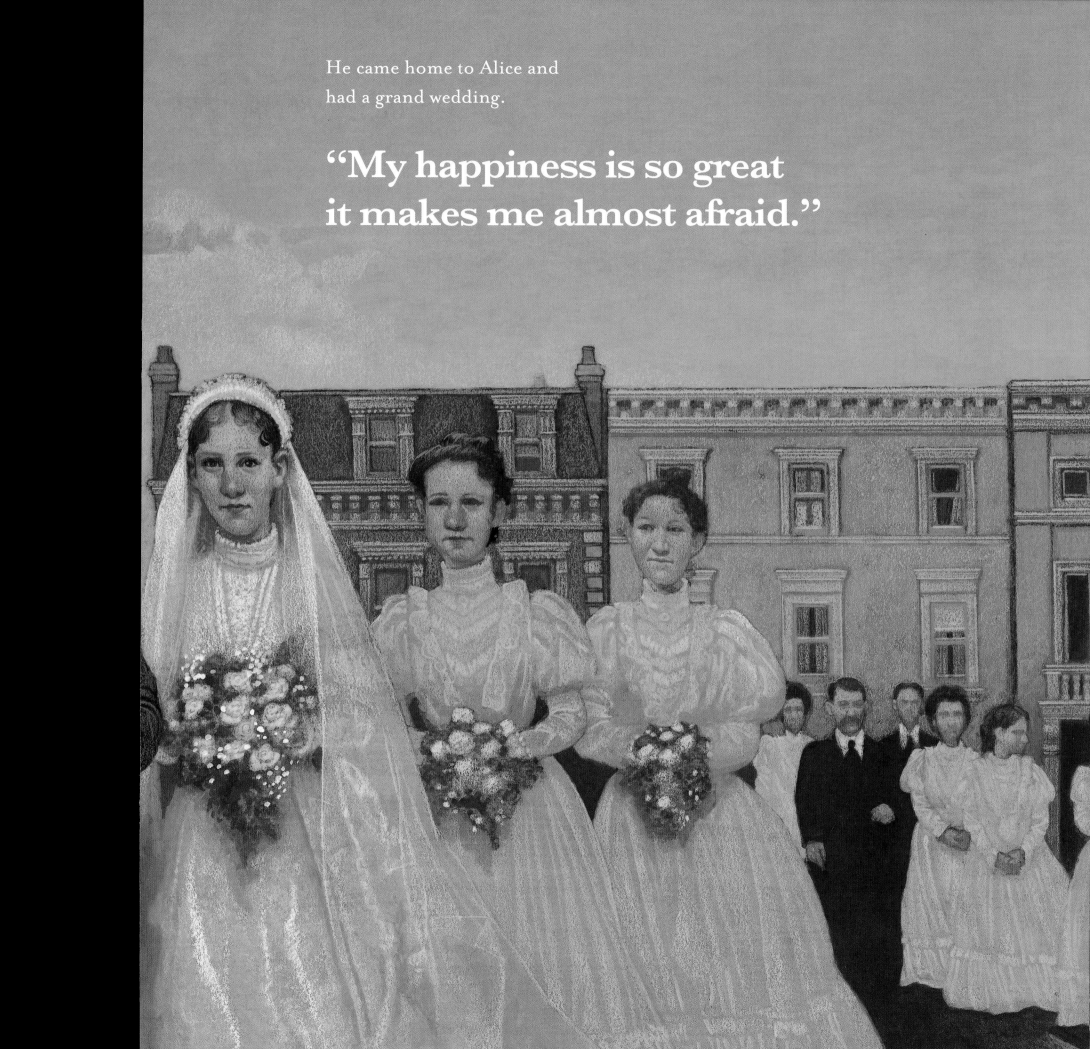

He came home to Alice and
had a grand wedding.

"My happiness is so great
it makes me almost afraid."

At twenty-three, he was elected
as the youngest member of the
New York State Assembly.
He wrote four bills in one week.
But he was new to politics,
and no one paid attention to him;
so he marched around the assembly yelling,
sometimes for forty minutes.
Many lawmakers did not like his ideas.
But they couldn't silence him.

"I would rather go out of politics
feeling that I had done right than stay,
knowing I have acted as I ought not to."

His bills didn't pass, but
he became a leader in the Republican Party.

"I rose like a rocket."

On February 12, 1884, Alice gave birth to their daughter.
Teddy's happiness turned to sorrow two days later
when both his wife and his mother unexpectedly died.

# "The light has gone out of my life."

He went back to work in a frenzy.

"Indeed I think I should go mad
if I were not employed."

But nothing stilled his sadness.

He left for the Dakota Territory to be

"far off from all mankind,"

leaving baby Alice Lee in the care of his sister Bamie.

He stayed almost three years,
hunting, raising cattle,
reading poetry, and writing books.

He returned East, muscular and healthy,
but still very sad.

Then love came into his life again with Edith Carow.

# "You have no idea how sweet Edith is,"
he wrote his sister.

But news of vicious blizzards pulled
Teddy back to the Dakotas.
He saw how wildlife was disappearing
from too much hunting and building.

# "The land was a barren waste. Not a green thing could be seen."

He could not let this happen.
Teddy formed a group that lobbied Congress
to pass laws to protect California's sequoias
and Alaska's seals, salmon, and seabirds.

And while he was doing all this,
he was also writing more books.

At thirty-one, he was appointed
Civil Service Commissioner.
He investigated illegalities
in Indiana, Wisconsin, and Maryland.

## "We stirred things up well."

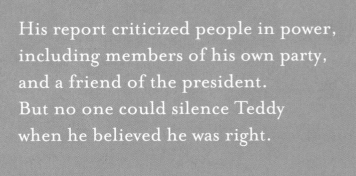

His report criticized people in power,
including members of his own party,
and a friend of the president.
But no one could silence Teddy
when he believed he was right.

## "An office holder must do his duty for the whole people, not for any party or any faction."

Many Republican lawmakers in the capital
sighed with relief when Teddy left to become
New York City's police commissioner.

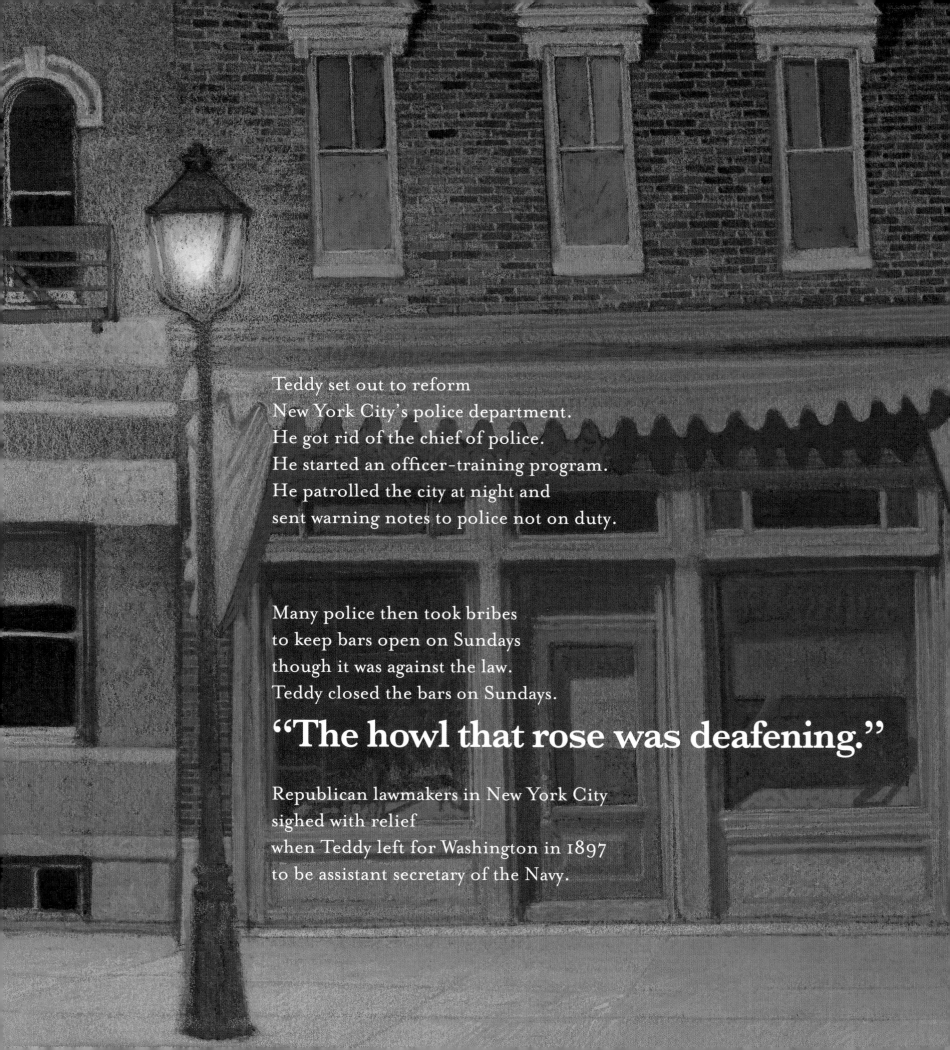

Teddy set out to reform
New York City's police department.
He got rid of the chief of police.
He started an officer-training program.
He patrolled the city at night and
sent warning notes to police not on duty.

Many police then took bribes
to keep bars open on Sundays
though it was against the law.
Teddy closed the bars on Sundays.

## "The howl that rose was deafening."

Republican lawmakers in New York City
sighed with relief
when Teddy left for Washington in 1897
to be assistant secretary of the Navy.

Teddy was convinced trouble was ahead
with Spain, which controlled Cuba.
He insisted the United States build more
battleships, cruisers, and torpedo boats.

On February 15, 1898,
when an American ship was blown up
in Cuba's harbor, Teddy declared:

# "It was sunk by an act of dirty treachery by the Spaniards."

It turned out he was wrong, but the
U.S. declared war on Spain anyway.
Teddy resigned from the navy and
joined the army.

In Cuba he found himself in charge of the First Volunteer Cavalry Regiment, nicknamed the Rough Riders.

*Charge!* Roosevelt ordered.

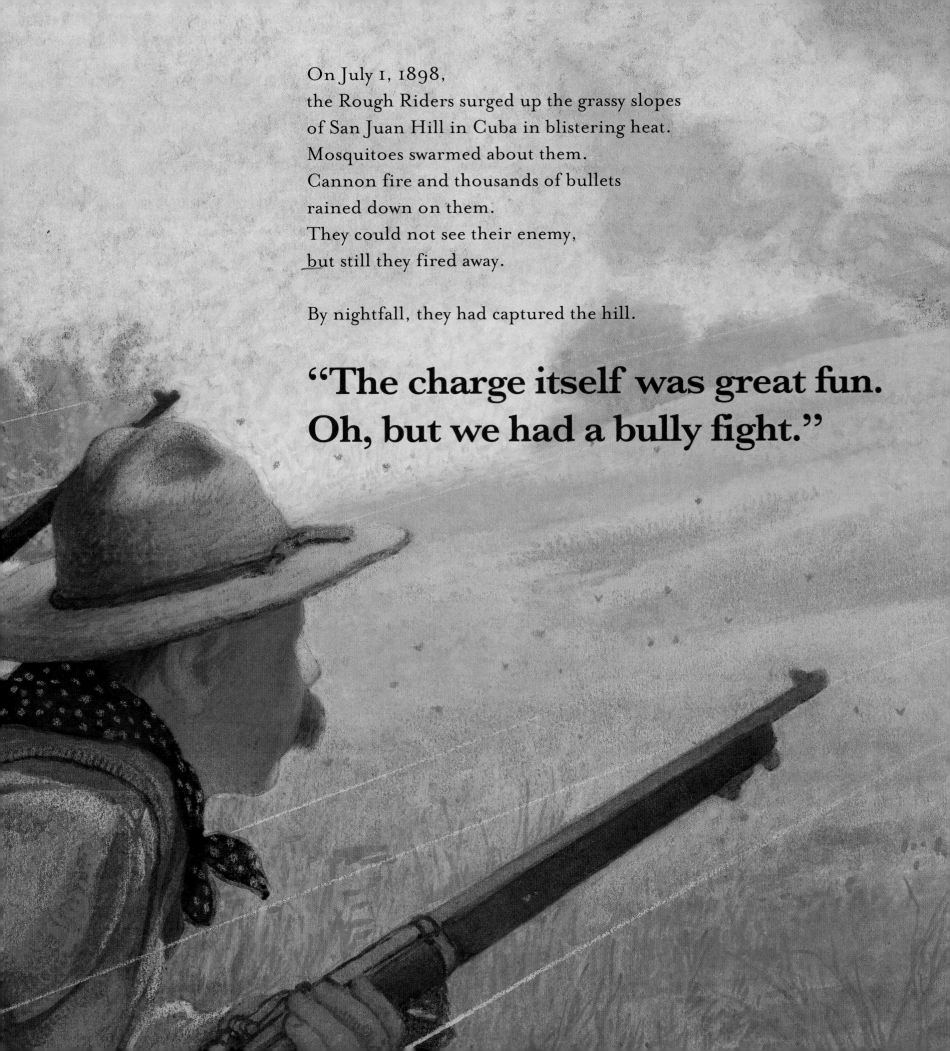

On July 1, 1898,
the Rough Riders surged up the grassy slopes
of San Juan Hill in Cuba in blistering heat.
Mosquitoes swarmed about them.
Cannon fire and thousands of bullets
rained down on them.
They could not see their enemy,
but still they fired away.

By nightfall, they had captured the hill.

**"The charge itself was great fun.
Oh, but we had a bully fight."**

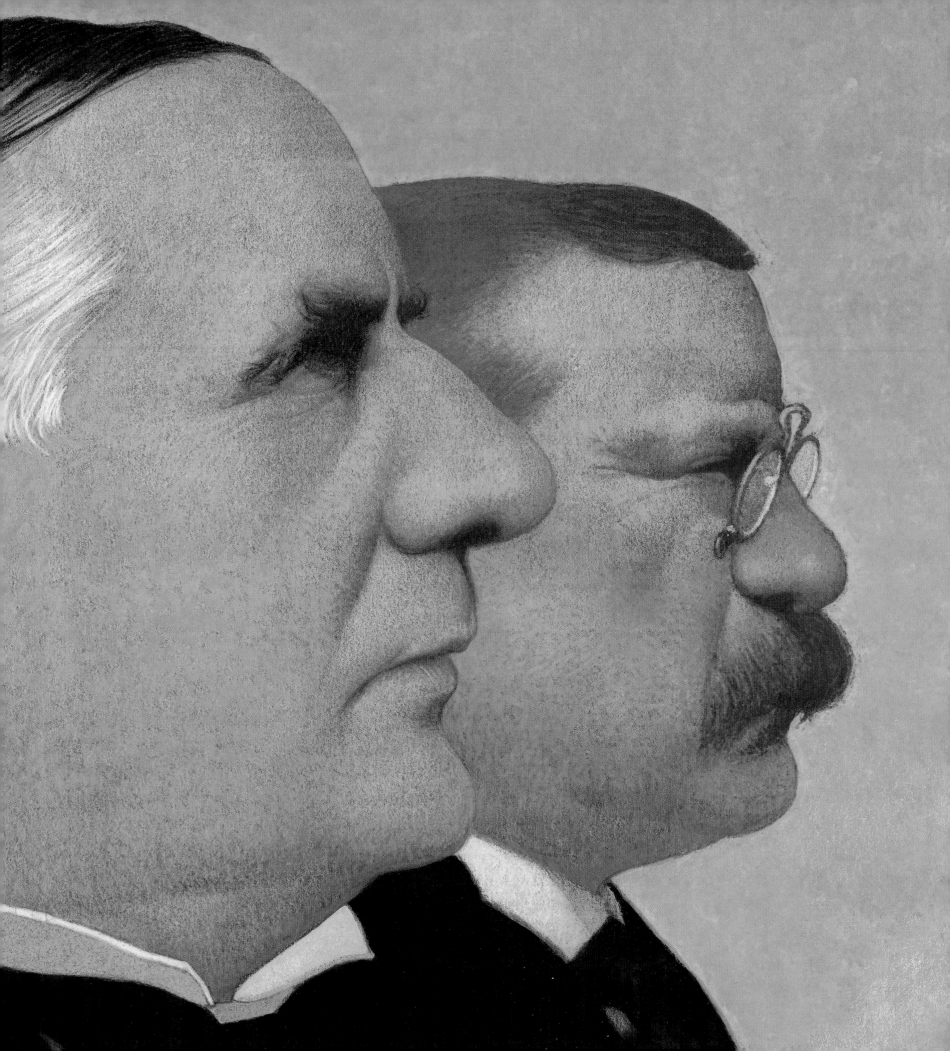

Teddy returned home a national hero.
Republican politicians all over the country,
seeing how famous he was,
urged him to run for governor of New York.
He did, and he won.

Republicans asked him to run
as William McKinley's vice president.
He thought the job would be too boring.

## "I could not do anything as Vice President; and yet I would be seeing continually things I would like to do."

He ran anyway.
McKinley won.

Nine months later,
McKinley was assassinated
and Roosevelt became president.

Teddy, Edith, and their six children
moved with their guinea pigs, ponies,
badgers, parrots, dogs, and snakes
into the White House.
His children raced about their new home
on stilts, roller skates, and bicycles.
His daughter Alice liked sliding down the banister
in an evening gown to greet visitors.

# "Children make all other forms of success lose their importance by comparison."

Early morning found the president
galloping about the capital on horseback,
or hanging from a cable to strengthen his wrists,
or staring at birds in trees.
Then came a whirl of meetings with
advisors, lawmakers, and reporters.
Evenings often ended with
pillow fights, wrestling matches,
and throwing water balloons off the roof.
Edith said that Teddy was her seventh child.

Business in America was booming.
But small companies could not compete
with big companies called trusts.
Roosevelt thought this unfair.
He sued a railroad trust.
He won and broke up the railroad trust.
Then he sued forty-four other trusts.
He created a new bureau, with rules for businesses.

# "Our aim is to control business, not strangle it."

Roosevelt was called a "trust buster."
He didn't like that term, but it stuck.

Roosevelt wanted a "Square Deal"
for all Americans, rich and poor.
He spoke out against children working.
But he could not convince lawmakers
to rewrite those laws.
He helped settle a mining strike.
He pushed for new laws to end
unsanitary working conditions in
meatpacking and food plants
and to ban impure food and drugs.

Many Republican leaders disapproved of Teddy's actions.

# "I acted for the well-being of all our people."

But most Americans liked
what Teddy did and said.
They elected him in a landslide
when he ran for his own term in 1904.

There was still work to be done
to save America's natural resources.
Too many forests were gone,
chopped down for timber and money.
Sheep growers had overgrazed their land.
Farmers had overplanted their fields.
Irrigation was desperately needed.
National monuments were crumbling
and had to be saved too.

## "We are not building this country for a day.  It is to last through the ages."

As president, Roosevelt created
eighteen national monuments,
fifty national forests,
fifty-one bird reservations,
four national game preserves,
five  national parks,
and twenty-four reclamation projects,
saving 230 million acres.

"There can be no greater issue
than that of conservation
in this country."

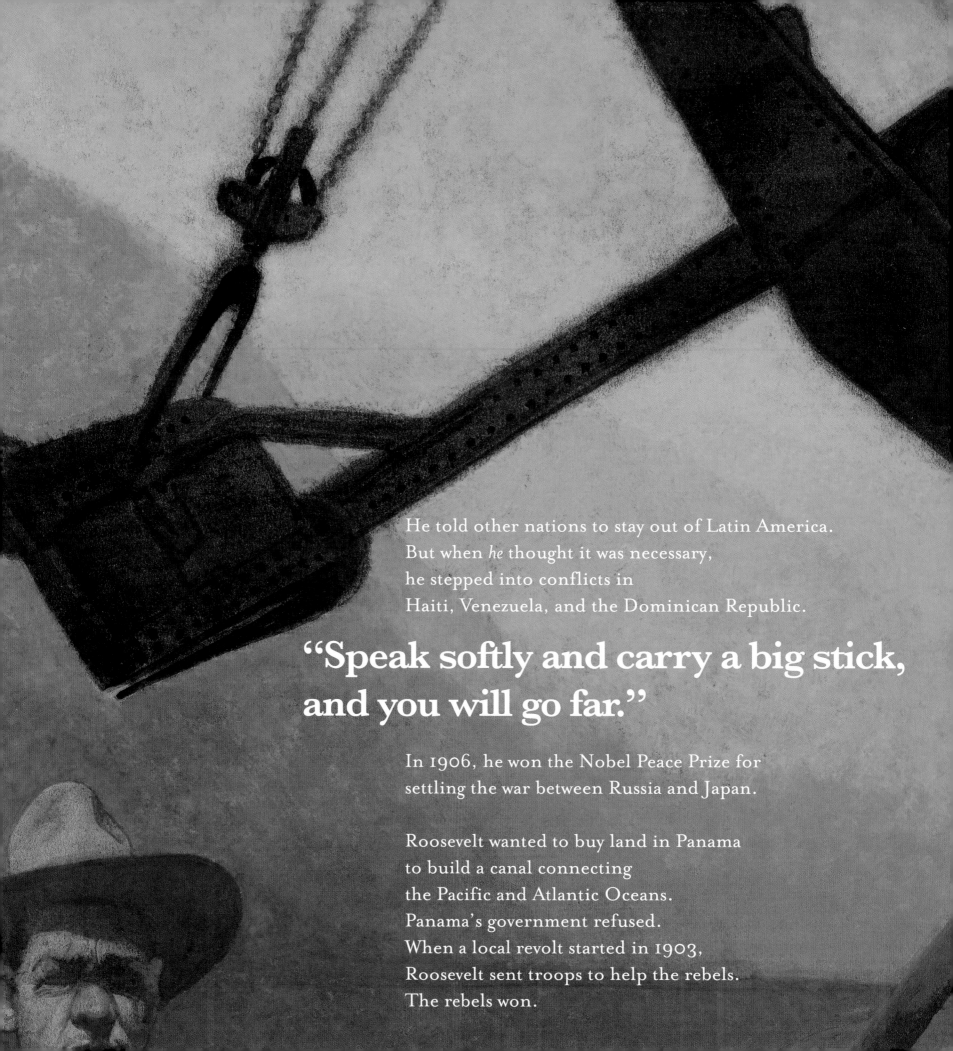

He told other nations to stay out of Latin America.
But when *he* thought it was necessary,
he stepped into conflicts in
Haiti, Venezuela, and the Dominican Republic.

## "Speak softly and carry a big stick, and you will go far."

In 1906, he won the Nobel Peace Prize for
settling the war between Russia and Japan.

Roosevelt wanted to buy land in Panama
to build a canal connecting
the Pacific and Atlantic Oceans.
Panama's government refused.
When a local revolt started in 1903,
Roosevelt sent troops to help the rebels.
The rebels won.

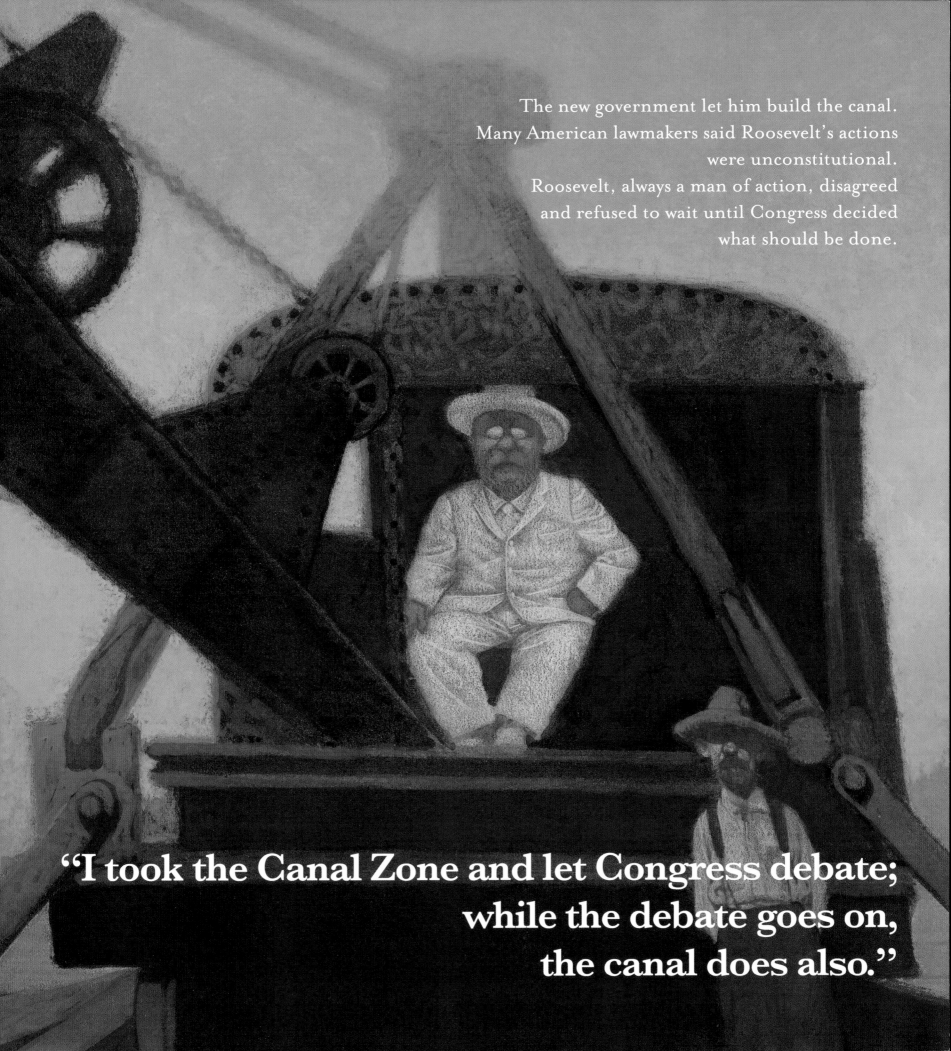

The new government let him build the canal.
Many American lawmakers said Roosevelt's actions
were unconstitutional.
Roosevelt, always a man of action, disagreed
and refused to wait until Congress decided
what should be done.

"I took the Canal Zone and let Congress debate;
while the debate goes on,
the canal does also."

Roosevelt decided not to run for a third term.
But that didn't mean he was going to stay home and rest.
He went to Africa to hunt and
collect specimens.
Returning home, he was so unhappy
about what the Republicans were saying,
that he formed a new political party:
the Progressive Bull Moose Party.

In 1912 he ran for president again.
He lost.

# "It is hard to fail, but it is worse never to have tried to succeed."

Teddy Roosevelt lived until he was sixty-one.

# "No man has had a happier life than I have led; a happier life in every way."

# Important Events

**October 27, 1858** Theodore Roosevelt was born to Theodore and Martha ("Mittie") Bulloch Roosevelt in New York City.

**1860** Elliott Roosevelt is born.

**1861** Corinne Roosevelt is born.

**1869** Theodore starts a physical fitness regimen.

**May 1870** The Roosevelt family tours Europe. Two years later they take a second trip abroad.

**1876–1880** Theodore attends and graduates with honors from Harvard.

**October 27, 1880** Theodore marries Alice Hathaway Lee.

**November 1881–1884** He serves in the New York State Assembly, becoming minority leader in 1883.

**1883** He hunts in the Dakota Territory and buys land for cattle ranching.

**February 12, 1884** Alice Lee is born. Two days later, his wife Alice and his mother die.

**December 1886** He marries Edith Carow. They have five children: Theodore, 1887; Kermit, 1889; Ethel, 1891; Archibald, 1894; Quentin, 1897.

**May 1889–May 1895** Roosevelt serves as U.S. Civil Service Commissioner.

**May 1895–April 1897** TR is the president of the Board of Police Commissioners in New York City.

**1897–1898** TR serves as assistant secretary of the Navy.

**April 23, 1898** Congress declares war against Spain over Cuba.

**May 15–September 16, 1898** He serves with First U.S. Volunteer Cavalry Regiment, the "Rough Riders," during the Spanish-American War.

**November 8, 1899–December 31, 1900** TR is governor of New York State.

**November 6, 1900** TR is elected vice president of the United States.

**September 14, 1901** He is sworn in as the twenty-sixth president.

**February 19, 1902** TR orders an antitrust suit under the Sherman Act, the first of forty-five antitrust suits.

**October 15, 1902** TR settles the Anthracite Coal Strike.

**December 31, 1902** Roosevelt settles the Venezuelan Affair.

**May 22, 1902–1909** TR launches his conservation, reclamation, and monument projects.

**February 1903** The Department of Commerce and Labor is established.

**November 18, 1903** Roosevelt signs a treaty to build the Panama Canal, which is completed in 1914.

**November 1904** TR is elected president in a landslide.

**June 29, 1906** TR signs the Hepburn Act, giving the Interstate Commerce Commission power to regulate railroad rates.

**June 30, 1906** TR signs Pure Food and Drug Act and Federal Meat Inspection Law.

**1906** TR becomes the first American to win the Nobel Peace Prize.

**1912** Roosevelt runs for president on the Bull Moose Party ticket but loses.

**1913–1914** He goes on a hunting and specimen-collecting excursion in South America.

**July 14, 1918** Quentin Roosevelt, Teddy's youngest son, dies in aerial combat during World War I.

**January 6, 1919** Theodore Roosevelt dies at home.

## Selected Research Sources

McCullough, David G. *Mornings on Horseback*. New York: Simon and Schuster, 1981.

——*The Path Between the Seas: The Creation of the Panama Canal, 1870–1914*. New York: Simon and Schuster, 1977.

Millard, Candace. *The River of Doubt: Theodore Roosevelt's Darkest Journey*. New York: Doubleday, 2005.

Morris, Edmund. *Colonel Roosevelt*. New York: Random House, 2010.

——*The Rise of Theodore Roosevelt*. New York: Coward, McCann and Geoghegan, 1979.

——*Theodore Rex*. New York: Random House, 2001.

Roosevelt, Theodore. *An Autobiography*. New York, Scribner, 1913.

——*African Game Trails*. New York: Scribner, 1910.

——*The Rough Riders*. New York: Scribner, 1898.

Sinclair, Upton. *The Jungle*. New York: Doubleday, Page, 1906.

## If you want to learn more about Theodore Roosevelt, you can read:

### Books:

Brown, Don. *Teedie: The Story of Young Teddy Roosevelt*. Boston: Houghton Mifflin Books for Children, 2009.

Fritz, Jean. *Bully for You, Teddy Roosevelt!* Unforgettable Americans series. Illustrated by Mike Wimmer. New York: Puffin, 1997.

Kraft, Betsy Harvey. *Theodore Roosevelt: Champion of the American Spirit*. New York: Clarion Books, 2003.

Wadsworth, Ginger. *Camping with the President*. Illustrated by Karen Dugan. Honesdale, Pa.: Boyds Mills Press, 2009.

### Websites:

"About Theodore Roosevelt—26th President and Much More…" www.theodoreroosevelt.org

"The History of Teddy's Bear" www.nps.gov/thri/forkids/teddybearhistory.htm

Sagamore Hill National Historic Site www.nps.gov/sahi

Theodore Roosevelt and Conservation www.nps.gov/thro/historyculture/theodore-roosevelt-and-conservation.htm

Theodore Roosevelt Association www.theodoreroosevelt.org and www.theodoreroosevelt.org/kidscorner/tr_teddy.htm

Theodore Roosevelt Birthplace National Historic Site www.nps.gov/thrb

Theodore Roosevelt National Park, North Dakota www.nps.gov/thro/index.htm

Theodore Roosevelt Tour, American Museum of Natural History www.amnh.org/plan-your-visit/popular-tours/theodore-roosevelt-tour

"I don't think any President ever enjoyed himself more than I did.

Moreover, I don't think any ex-President ever enjoyed himself more."